Competitive Programming:

Java and C++

(Questions and Solutions), Vol. 1

By:
Department of Computer Science
Faculty of Computer & Mathematical Sciences
Universiti Teknologi MARA Perlis Branch
Malaysia

Editorial Committee
Mahfudzah Othman
Muhammad Nabil Fikri Jamaluddin
Alif Faisal Ibrahim

Authors
Assoc Prof Dr Naimah Mohd Hussin
Mahfudzah Othman
Jamal Othman
Nora Yanti Che Jan
Nurzaid Muhd Zain
Mohd Nizam Osman
Hawa Mohd Ekhsan
Jiwa Noris Hamid
Umi Hanim Mazlan
Hanisah Ahmad
Muhammad Nabil Fikri Jamaluddin
Alif Faisal Ibrahim

ISBN: 978-0-359-66521-1

PREFACE

Competitive Programming can be defined as a mind sport, where the competitions usually held over the Internet or Local Area Network. Participants are called "sport programmers" where they need to program based on the provided tasks.

Since 2011, the Department of Computer Science, Faculty of Computer and Mathematical Science, Universiti Teknologi MARA Perlis Branch has been organising Competitive Programming competitions every year, nationally and internationally. These competitions, which are called as CPROM and COPSCOM, were held yearly to discover students' potential in C++ and Java programming. Over the past eight years, the lecturers from Computer Science Department have been working together to come out with programming tasks or questions to be solved by the participants. The questions, ranging from easy to hard questions require high cognitive ability among participants. Regardless of the differents levels of complexity of the questions, most of the participants seemed to improve their problem-solving skills, acquired higher logical and reasoning abilities and improved their interests and motivations in Java and C++ programming.

This book is the compilation of the questions and possible solutions in Java and C++ from the competitions held from year 2011 until now. It is hoped that the book can help students to improve their problem-solving and coding skills in Java and C++ programming.

Department of Computer Science
Faculty of Computer and Mathematical Sciences
Universiti Teknologi MARA
Perlis Branch
MALAYSIA

TABLE OF CONTENTS

CHAPTER 1:
COMPETITIVE PROGRAMMING,QUESTIONS & ANSWERS
(Solutions in Java)

CHAPTER 2:
COMPETITIVE PROGRAMMING,QUESTIONS & ANSWERS
(Solutions in C++)

CHAPTER 1:

COMPETITIVE PROGRAMMING
QUESTIONS & ANSWERS
(Solutions in Java)

PROBLEM 1 : STATISTICS

The coordinator plans to prepare a statistic from the recent examination. The statistic will be presented during the meeting to report the performance of the students.

Your task is to write a program that reads the student's marks from each class and print the report as required.

Input
The first line of input is an Integer number (1 ≤ N ≤ 10) which indicate the number of classes. The next line consists of data for the first class whereby the first data indicates total students and followed by the list of marks obtained by each students seperated by a single space. This repeats until the last class.

Output
The report of the result will be the ascending order of the marks for each class and ends with the highest mark obtained by the student at each line.

Sample Input	Sample Output
2 5 45 23 65 76 21 7 95 63 77 59 39 63 76	21 23 45 65 76 76 39 59 63 63 76 77 95 95

POSSIBLE SOLUTION: STATISTICS (*Java*)

```java
import java.io.*;
import java.util.*;

public class CPROMQ4 {
    public static void main (String[] args) {
        Scanner scan = new Scanner (System.in);
        int N = scan.nextInt ();

        int[] totStud = new int[10];
        int[][] marks = new int[10][10];

        for (int i=1; i<= N; i++) {
            totStud[i] = scan.nextInt ();

            for (int j=1;j<=totStud[i];j++){
                marks[i][j] = scan.nextInt ();
            }
        }
        for (int i=1; i<= N; i++) {
        int highest = 0;

            for (int j=1;j<=totStud[i];j++) {
                if (marks[i][j] > highest)
                    highest = marks[i][j];
            }

            for (int j=1;j<=totStud[i];j++) {
                for (int k = 1 ;k<=totStud[i] - 1; k++ ) {
                    if (marks[i][k] > marks[i][k+1])
                        {
                            int temp = marks[i][k];
                            marks[i][k] = marks[i][k+1];
                            marks[i][k+1] = temp;
                        }
                }
            }

            for (int j=1;j<=totStud[i];j++)
                System.out.print(marks[i][j]+" ");

            System.out.print(highest);
            System.out.print("\n");
        }
    }//close main
}//close class
```

PROBLEM 2 : PALINDROME

A palindrome is a word, phrase, number or other sequence of units (such as a strand of DNA) that has the property of reading the same in either direction (the adjustment of punctuation and spaces between words is generally permitted).

Examples of palindrome are as follows :-
mom
dad
tattarrattat
rotator
reviver

Input
The first line of the input contains an integer N (1 ≤ N ≤ 5), the number of test cases. Following the first line are the test cases. Each line in a test case contains a word, phrase or numbers.

The input must be read from standard input.

Output
The output of the program should print either the word is **Palindrome** or **Not Palindrome**.

The output must be written to standard output.

Sample Input	Sample Output
4 repaper madam woow madam adinda 12344321	Palindrome Palindrome Not Palindrome Palindrome

POSSIBLE SOLUTION: PALINDROME (*Java*)

```java
import java.io.*;
import java.util.*;

public class CPROMQ2 {
      public static void main (String[] args) {

            Scanner scan = new Scanner (System.in);
            String lineSeparator = System.getProperty("line.separator");
            scan.useDelimiter(lineSeparator);

            String[] word_sentence = new String[10];

            int N = scan.nextInt();

            for (int a = 1; a<= N; a++) {
                word_sentence[a] = scan.next();
            }

            for (int a = 1; a<= N; a++) {

                int len = word_sentence[a].length();
                int divide = len / 2 ;

                int sama = 0;

                for (int i=0;i<divide;i++) {
                    if(word_sentence[a].charAt(i)==word_sentence[a].charAt(len
                    - i - 1))
                        sama++;
                }

                if (sama == divide)
                    System.out.println("Palindrom");
                else
                    System.out.println("Not Palindrome");
            }


      }//close main
}//close class
```

PROBLEM 3 : CONSONANTS & VOWELS

A word consists of consonants and vowels. Do you realized that some words have more vowels than the consonants. Your tasks is to enter a word and count number of vowels and consonants in the word.

Input
The first line of the input contains an integer N ($1 \leq N \leq 5$), the number of test cases. Following the first line are the test cases. Each line of a test case contains a string data.

The input must be read from standard input.

Output
The output of the program should display the total of vowels and consonants in the word.

The output must be written to standard output.

Sample Input	Sample Output
3 sequoia rhythm fuyooo	5 2 0 6 4 2

POSSIBLE SOLUTION: CONSONANTS & VOWELS (*Java*)

```java
import java.util.*;

public class cprom_prob1 {
    public static void main(String[] args) {
        Scanner scan = new Scanner (System.in);
        String lineSeparator = System.getProperty("line.separator");
        scan.useDelimiter(lineSeparator);

        int N = 0;
        System.out.println("Enter number of test cases : ");
        N = scan.nextInt();

        String[] word = new String[10];

        for (int i=0;i<N;i++) {
            word[i] = scan.next();
        }

        for (int i=0;i<N;i++){
            int m = word[i].length();
            int countVowels=0;
            int countConsonants=0;
            for (int x=0;x<m;x++){
                if ((word[i].substring(x,x+1).equalsIgnoreCase("a"))
                  ||(word[i].substring(x,x+1).equalsIgnoreCase("e"))
                  ||(word[i].substring(x,x+1).equalsIgnoreCase("i"))
                  ||(word[i].substring(x,x+1).equalsIgnoreCase("o"))
                  ||(word[i].substring(x,x+1).equalsIgnoreCase("u")))
                {
                            countVowels++;
                 }
                else
                    countConsonants++;
            }

            System.out.println(countVowels+" "+countConsonants);
            countVowels=0;
            countConsonants=0;
        }

    }//close main
}//close class
```

PROBLEM 4 : MAGIC SQUARES

A magic square is a two-dimensional arrangement of positive integers with a special property: All rows, columns and diagonals total the same number. Below, for example, the 3-by-3 arrangement of nine (9) numbers is a magic square:

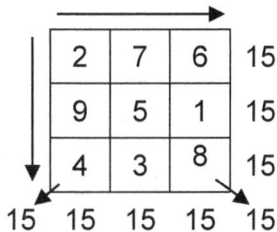

Your assignment is to read a square of numbers as input and determine whether it is a magic square or not.

Input

The first line will contain a positive integer $2 < N < 6$, which represents the number of columns and rows in the square. The next N lines will each contains N positive integers separated by spaces.

The input must be read from standard input.

Output

The output of the program should print the result, either **MAGIC** or **NO**.

The output must be written to standard output.

Sample Input	Sample Output
3 2 7 6 9 5 1 4 3 8	MAGIC
3 1 2 3 4 5 6 7 8 9	No

POSSIBLE SOLUTION: MAGIC SQUARES (*Java*)

```java
import java.util.*;
import java.io.*;

public class Magic {

    public static void main(String[] args) {
        Scanner scan = new Scanner(System.in);
        Scanner scanN = new Scanner(System.in);
        String lineSeparator = System.getProperty("line.separator");
        scan.useDelimiter(lineSeparator);

        int N = scanN.nextInt();

        String[] data = new String[N];


        for (int i=0; i<N; i++)
        {
            data[i] = scan.nextLine();
        }

        System.out.println("\n\n");

        int [][] sqr = new int[N][N];
        for(int i=0; i<N; i++)//outer FOR to control each of input
        {
            StringTokenizer st = new StringTokenizer(data[i]);
            int cntToken = st.countTokens();

            for(int j=0; j<N; j++)
                sqr[i][j] = Integer.parseInt(st.nextToken());
        }

        int tot = 0;
        for (int c=0; c<N; c++)
            tot += sqr[c][0];

        //Process board: ROWS
        for (int row=0; row<N; row++){
            int sum = 0;
            for(int i=0; i<N; i++)
                sum += sqr[row][i];



            if (sum != tot){
                System.out.println("NO");
                System.exit(0);
```

```java
            }
        }
        //Process board: COLUMNS
        for (int col=0; col<N; col++){
            int sum = 0;
            for(int i=0; i<N; i++)
                 sum += sqr[i][col];

            if (sum != tot){
                 System.out.println("NO");
                 System.exit(0);
            }
        }
        //Process board: DIAGONALS
        int sum1 =0, sum2 =0;
        for(int col=0; col<N; col++ ){
            sum1 += sqr[col][col];
            sum2 += sqr[N-col-1][col];
        }
        if (sum1 != tot){
                 System.out.println("NO");
            System.exit(0);
        }
        if (sum2 != tot){
            System.out.println("NO");
            System.exit(0);
        }
        System.out.println("MAGIC");
    }
}
```

PROBLEM 5: TIME CLOCK

You need to compute the total time a worker has worked on a single calendar day given two timestamps of the form "HH:MM". The numbers MM can be in the range of "00" to "59" while HH is in the range "01" through "12". This is an archaic (old-fashioned) timestamp clock that doesn't even record AM or PM values. The system has worked well in the past because no-one has ever worked longer than an 8 hour shift.

You can be assured that the two times are different and represent an employee checking in to work (on a calendar day) and checking out from work later on the exact same calendar day. You are to output the total time as "HH:MM". If the accumulated work time is greater than 8 hours (in other words, 481 minutes or longer), then you are ordered to output "08:00" because this is the maximum time that the employee would be paid.

Input
The first line of the input contains an integer N (1 ≤ N ≤ 30), the number of test cases. The following line will contain pairs of timestamps representing the starting and ending time containing five characters of the form "HH:MM" where HH is in the range "01" and "12" while MM in the range "00" through "59".

The input must be read from standard input.

Output
The output of the program should display the accumulated time as "HH:MM" on a single line by itself where HH represents the number of hours in the range "00" to "12" and MM represents the number of minutes in the range "00" and "59".

The output must be written to standard output.

Sample Input	Sample Output
4	
09:13 04:42	07:29
09:12 10:03	00:51
03:10 11:15	08:00
07:13 01:01	05:48

POSSIBLE SOLUTION: TIME CLOCK (Java)

```java
import java.util.*;
import java.io.*;

public class Time {

    public static void main(String[] args) {
        Scanner scan = new Scanner(System.in);
        Scanner scanN = new Scanner(System.in);
        String lineSeparator = System.getProperty("line.separator");
        scan.useDelimiter(lineSeparator);

        int N = scanN.nextInt();

        String[] data = new String[N];

        for (int i=0; i<N; i++)
        {
            data[i] = scan.nextLine();
        }

        System.out.println("\n\n");

        for(int i=0; i<N; i++)
        {
            StringTokenizer st = new StringTokenizer(data[i]);

            String t1 = st.nextToken();
            String t2 = st.nextToken();

            int start = Integer.parseInt(t1.substring(0,2))*60 +
                        Integer.parseInt(t1.substring(3,5));
            int end = Integer.parseInt(t2.substring(0,2))*60 +
                        Integer.parseInt(t2.substring(3,5));

            if (end < start)
                end += 12*60;

            int totmm = end - start;

            if (totmm > 480)
                totmm = 480;

            int hh = totmm/60;

            if (hh<10)
                System.out.print("0");
```

```java
        System.out.print(hh);
        System.out.print(":");

        int mm = totmm - hh*60;
        if(mm<10)
            System.out.print("0");
        System.out.print(mm);
        System.out.println("\n\n");
    }

  }
}
```

PROBLEM 6: PALINDROME - Version 2

A positive integer is said to be a palindrome with respect to base b, if its representation in base b reads the same from left to right as from right to left. Palindromes are formed as follows:
Given a number, reverse its digits and add the resulting number to the original number. If the result isn't a palindrome, repeat the process. For example, start with 87 base 10. Applying this process, we obtain:

```
87 + 78 = 165
      165 + 561 = 726
            726 + 627 = 1353
                  1353 + 3531 = 4884, a palindrome
```

Whether all numbers eventually become palindromes under this process is unproved, but all base 10 numbers less than 10,000 have been tested. Every one becomes a palindrome in a relatively small number of steps (of the 900 3-digit numbers, 90 are palindromes to start with and 735 of the remainder take fewer than 5 reversals and additions to yield a palindrome). Except, that is, for 196. Although no proof exists that it will not produce a palindrome, this number has been carried through to produce a 2 million-digit number without producing a palindrome.

Input
The first line of the input contains an integer N (1 ≤ N ≤ 5), the number of test cases. Following the first line are the test cases. Each line of a test case contains an integer number. All test cases are non negative integer numbers.
The input must be read from standard input.

Output
Print the palindrome number produced and followed by for how many attempts the palindrome number is found. If no palindrome is produced after 10 attempts, print the last sum and the word "none".

Sample Input	Sample Output
5	
87	4884;Palindrome;5
196	10755470;None
1689	56265;Palindrome;5
46785	1552551;Palindrome;4
46894	664272356;None

13

POSSIBLE SOLUTION: PALINDROME- Version 2 *(Java)*

```java
import java.util.*;
public class cprom_prob4 {
    public static void main(String[] args){
        Scanner scan = new Scanner (System.in);
        int N = 0;

        System.out.println("Enter number of test cases : ");
        N = scan.nextInt();

        int[] numbers = new int[5];

        for (int i=0;i<N;i++){  numbers[i] = scan.nextInt();  }

        String reverse = "";
        String palin = "";
        int attempt = 0;
        int tot = 0;

        for (int i=0;i<N;i++){
            attempt = 0;
            boolean palindrome=false;
            String numX = ""+numbers[i];
            int leng = numX.length();
            int sama=0;

            for (int z=0;z<leng;z++){
                if (numX.charAt(z)==numX.charAt(leng-z-1))
                    sama++;
            }

            attempt++;
            if (sama==leng){
                palindrome = true;
                tot = Integer.parseInt(numX);
            }



            else {
                while (attempt != 10){
                    String tempNum = numX;
                        reverse = "";
                        leng = tempNum.length();
                        for (int y=leng-1;y>=0;y--){
                            reverse = reverse+tempNum.charAt(y);
                        }
                    int reverseNumb = Integer.parseInt(reverse);
                        int tNum = Integer.parseInt(tempNum);

                        tot = tNum + reverseNumb;
                        String totX = ""+tot;
                        int lengTotX = totX.length();
```

```
                         int samaTotX = 0;

                         for (int z=0;z<lengTotX;z++){
               if (totX.charAt(z)==totX.charAt(lengTotX-z-1))
                              samaTotX++;
                         }

                         attempt++;
                         numX = ""+tot;

                         if (samaTotX == lengTotX)      {
                              palindrome = true;
                              break;                    }
                    }//close while
               }//close else

               if (palindrome == true){
                    System.out.println(tot+";Palindrome;"+attempt);
               }
               else
                    System.out.println(tot+";None");
          }//close for
     }//close main
}//close class
```

PROBLEM 7 : DECODING ROMAN NUMERALS

The roman people uses the Roman Numerals for base 10 numbers. Each numeral-character such as I, V, X, L, C, D and M has a single value such as 1, 5, 10, 50, 100, 500 and 1000 respectively. The value of Roman Numerals is the sum of its numeral-characters unless a smaller numeral-character is placed in front of larger numeral-character, in which case the smaller numeral-character is subtracted from the total. For instance VI = 5 + 1, while IV = 5 – 1. You may assume that at most one subtraction is required per number.

Input
Input are in the form of text string for roman numerals, separated by a single space in a single line.

Output
For each roman numerals, print the number in base 10 numbers at a single line.

Sample Input	Sample Output
IV LXI CLV DI MDCLXVII	4 61 155 501 1667

POSSIBLE SOLUTION: DECODING ROMAN NUMERALS (*Java*)

```java
import java.io.*;

public class Roman {
    public static void main (String [] args) throws Exception {
                InputStreamReader isr = new
                InputStreamReader(System.in);
                BufferedReader reader = new BufferedReader(isr);
                String line = reader.readLine();
                String[] RNs = line.split("\\s+");

                for (int i = 0; i < RNs.length; i++)   {
                    int value = getRN(RNs[i]);
                    System.out.println(value);     }
    }

    static int getRN(String RN)
    {
        int total = 0;
        for (int i = 0; i < RN.length(); i++) {
            //check if this is a single char string
            if (i == (RN.length()-1)) {
                    total += getRNIntValue(RN.charAt(i));
                    break;
            }
            //else we have a multi value string
            //and need to check for less than
    if (getRNIntValue(RN.charAt(i)) < getRNIntValue(RN.charAt(i+1)))
       {
            //subtraction case, take difference, and bump counter
            total += getRNIntValue(RN.charAt(i+1)) -
                    getRNIntValue(RN.charAt(i));
                    i++;
            }
            else { //straight addition
                    total += getRNIntValue(RN.charAt(i));
            }
        }

        return total;
    }

    static int getRNIntValue (char RNChar) {
        int charValue = 0;
        if (RNChar == 'I')
            return 1;
        if (RNChar == 'V')
            return 5;
```

```
            if (RNChar == 'X')
                return 10;
            if (RNChar == 'L')
                return 50;
            if (RNChar == 'C')
                return 100;
            if (RNChar == 'D')
                return 500;
            if (RNChar == 'M')
                return 1000;

            //else unrecognized char, so return zero
            return charValue;
        }
}
```

PROBLEM 8 : BUILD A PYRAMID

Build a pyramid is not an easy job. But as a computer experts you are able to build a pyramid within a second. Your task is to enter a number and a character. The material of the pyramid is the character's entered while the height of the pyramid is the number's entered.

Input
The first line of the input contains an integer N (1 ≤ N ≤ 5), the number of test cases. Following the first line are the test cases. Each line of a test case contains a non-negative integer number and a character separated by a single space. The non-negative number is smaller than 10 and the character is could be a number, alphabet or symbol.

The input must be read from standard input.

Output
The output of the program should display the design of the pyramid.

The output must be written to standard output.

Sample Input	Sample Output
3 2 * 5 ^ 3 @	

POSSIBLE SOLUTION: BUILD A PYRAMID (*Java*)

```java
import java.io.*;
import java.util.*;

public class CPROMQ1 {
    public static void main (String[] args) {

        Scanner scan = new Scanner (System.in);

        int N = scan.nextInt();

        int[] number = new int[10];
        String[] character = new String[10];

        for (int a = 1; a<= N; a++) {

        number[a] = scan.nextInt();

        character[a] = scan.next();
        }

        System.out.print("\n\n\n\n\n");

        for (int a = 1; a<= N; a++) {

        for (int i=1;i<=number[a];i++){

            for (int j = number[a] - 1;j>=i;j--){
                System.out.print(" ");
            }

            for (int k=1;k<=i;k++){
                System.out.print(character[a]);
                System.out.print(" ");
            }

            System.out.print("\n");
        }
            System.out.print("\n\n\n");

        }

    }//close main
}//close class
```

PROBLEM 9: COUNT THE KEYWORD

To find out and count manually the keyword in the passage is not easy. Imagine if the passage is more than 10 pages and you have to read through the whole passage from the first page until at the end of the passage but the keyword that you search is not found. You will be frustrated. As an expert in computer programming you are required to write a program to find and count how many times the keyword repeats in the passage.

Input
The first line of input is an Integer number (1 ≤ N ≤ 10) which indicate the test cases (number of passages). The second line is the keyword (String). Following the second line are the test cases. Each line in a test case contains a word, phrase or passage.

The input must be read from standard input.

Output
The output is either YES or NO and followed by how many times the keyword found in the passage.

Sample Input	Sample Output
4 Computer Yesterday i bought 2 computers and ipad. Computer and commuter are different things. Computer Sciences and Computer Multimedia. Bachelor in Business Computing.	YES 1 YES 1 YES 2 NO 0

POSSIBLE SOLUTION: COUNT THE KEYWORD (*Java*)

```java
import java.io.*;
import java.util.Scanner;

public class CPROMQ5 {
    public static void main (String[] args) {

        Scanner scan = new Scanner (System.in);
        scan.useDelimiter(System.getProperty("line.separator"));

        int N = scan.nextInt();
        String[] sentence = new String[10];
        String searchWord = scan.next();

        for (int a = 1; a<= N; a++)
            sentence[a] = scan.next();

        for (int a = 1; a<= N; a++) {
            int lenSentence = sentence[a].length();

            String found = "No";
            int count = 0;
            for (int x=0;x<lenSentence - searchWord.length();x++)
            {
                String word = "";

                for (int k=x;k<x+searchWord.length();k++) {
                    word = word +
                    Character.toString(sentence[a].charAt(k));
                }

                if (searchWord.equalsIgnoreCase(word)) {
                    found = "Yes";
                    count++;
                }

            }

            System.out.print(found+ " "+count);
            System.out.println();

        }

    }//close main
}//close class
```

PROBLEM 10: COMPUTATION OF MULTIPLICATION

Computes the multiplication of numbers between the two integers (both are inclusive) and the result of the multiplication is divided by 6. The two numbers could be a negative or positive numbers.

Input
The first line of the input contains an integer N (1 ≤ N ≤ 5), the number of test cases. Following the first line are the test cases. Each line in a test case contains a pair of Integer numbers seperated by a space.

The input must be read from standard input.

Output
The output of the program should print the result of the multiplication which divided by 6 and print 0 otherwise.

The output must be written to standard output.

Sample Input	Sample Output
3 3 5 10 11 -3 -1	60 0 -6

POSSIBLE SOLUTION: COMPUTATION OF MULTIPLICATION (*Java*)

```java
import java.io.*;
import java.util.*;

public class CPROMQ3 {
    public static void main (String[] args) {

        Scanner scan = new Scanner (System.in);
        int N = scan.nextInt();

        int[] num1 = new int[10];
        int[] num2 = new int[10];

        for (int a = 1; a<= N; a++) {
            num1[a] = scan.nextInt();
            num2[a] = scan.nextInt();
        }

        for (int a = 1; a<= N; a++) {

            int mul = 1;
            if (num1[a] < num2[a]) {
                for (int i=num1[a] ; i<=num2[a] ; i++){
                    mul = mul * i;
                }

                if (mul % 6 == 0)
                    System.out.println(mul);
                else
                    System.out.println("0");
            }

            if (num1[a] > num2[a]) {
                for (int i=num1[a] ; i>=num2[a] ; i--){
                    mul = mul * i;
                }

                if (mul % 6 == 0)
                    System.out.println(mul);
                else
                    System.out.println("0");
            }

        }
    }//close main
}//close class
```

CHAPTER 2:

COMPETITIVE PROGRAMMING
QUESTIONS & ANSWERS
(Solutions in C++)

PROBLEM 1 : DIVISIBLE NUMBERS

In mathematics, "divisible by" means when you divide one number by another number, the result is a whole number. In other words, the remaining balance of the division is zero (0).

For example, 10 is divisible by 2 and 5.

Input

The first line of the input contains the number of test cases which entered by user. Following the first line are the test cases. Each line in a test case contains two non-negative integer number where:

The first number represents the starting point of number in a series.
The second number represents the end point of number in a series.

For example,

20 30 means the series number starts from 20 and ends at 30.

The input must be read from standard input.

Output

The output of the program should print the numbers in the series that can be divisible by 4 and 6.

The output must be written to standard output.

Sample Input	Sample Output
3 10 50 80 120 100 150	12 24 36 48 84 96 108 120 108 120 132 144

POSSIBLE SOLUTION: DIVISIBLE NUMBERS *(C++)*

```cpp
#include <iostream>
using namespace std;

int main(void)
{
    int num;

    cin>>num;           //the number of cases
    int start[num], end[num];

    for (int i=0; i< num; i++)
    {
        cin>>start[i];      //starting integer
        cin>>end[i];        //the last integer
    }
     for (int i=0; i< num; i++)
    {
         for (int j=start[i]; j<=end[i]; j++)
         {
            if (j % 4 == 0 && j % 6 == 0)
                cout<<j<<" ";
         }
        cout<<endl;
    }
    system("pause");
}
```

PROBLEM 2 : SEQUENTIAL NUMBERS

The sequential numbers are the numbers which are sorted with special order. For instance the numbers 1, 2, 3 ... 8, 9, 10 are started with the number 1 and ends with the number 10. Difference of the current number and the next number is 1. The code obtains the first number, final number and difference of the current number with the next number as input.

Input
The first line of the input contains an integer N ($1 \le N \le 5$), the number of test cases. Following the first line are the test cases. Each line of a test case contains 3 integer numbers separated by a single space. The third number is non-negative integer number.

The input must be read from standard input.

Output
The output of the program should display as shown at below.
The output must be written to standard output.

Sample Input	Sample Output
3 1 10 1 90 9 9 -50 100 50	 1 2 3 4 5 6 7 8 9 10 90 81 72 63 54 45 36 27 18 9 -50 0 50 100

POSSIBLE SOLUTION: SEQUENTIAL NUMBERS *(C++)*

```cpp
#include <iostream.h>
#include <conio.h>

int main()
{
    int N=0;
    int firNum[5];
    int finNum[5];
    int dif[5];

    cout << "\n Enter total number of tests : ";
    cin >> N;

    for (int x=0;x<N;x++){
        cin >> firNum[x] >> finNum[x] >> dif[x];
    }

    for (int x=0;x<N;x++){
        if (firNum[x] < finNum[x]){
            for (int y=firNum[x];y<=finNum[x];y=y+dif[x])
                cout << y << "\t";
        }

        if (firNum[x] > finNum[x]){
            for (int y=firNum[x];y>=finNum[x];y=y-dif[x])
                cout << y << "\t";
        }
        cout << endl;
    }
 getche();
}
```

PROBLEM 3: FIND THE SHADED AREA

Given the diagram below, you are required to find the shaded area.

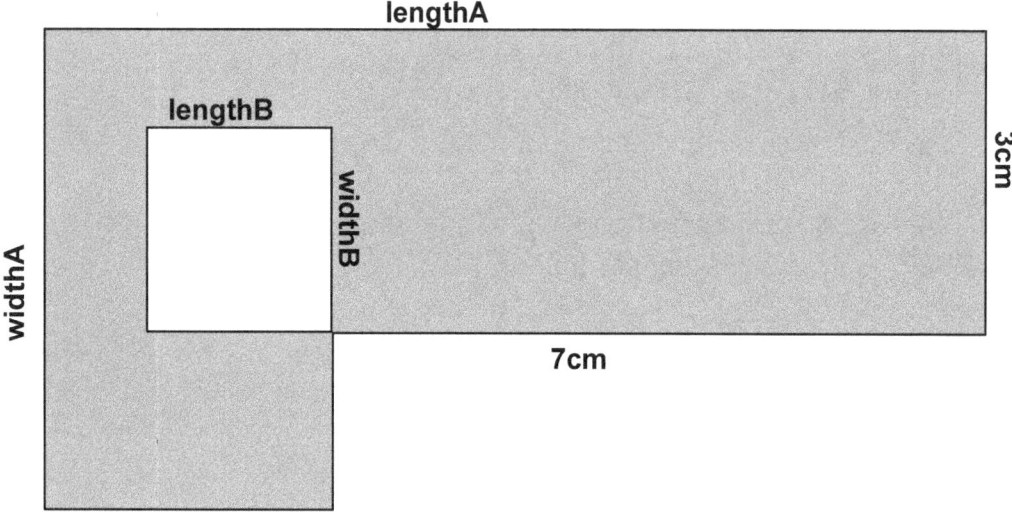

Input

The first line of the input contains the length and width of the outer shape. Followed by the length and width of the inner shape.

Output

The output will print the area of the outer and inner shapes and the shaded area.

Sample Input	Sample Output
10 5 2 2	36 4 32

POSSIBLE SOLUTION: FIND THE SHADED AREA *(C++)*

```cpp
#include<iostream>
using namespace std;

int main()
{
    int lengthA, widthA, lengthB, widthB, area_inner, area_outer,
area_shaded;

    cin>>lengthA>>widthA;
    cin>>lengthB>>widthB;

    area_outer = (lengthA * 3) + ((widthA - 3)*(lengthA - 7));
    area_inner = lengthB * widthB;
    area_shaded = area_outer - area_inner;

    cout<<area_outer<<endl;
    cout<<area_inner<<endl;
    cout<<area_shaded<<endl;

     system("pause");
}
```

PROBLEM 4 : FACTORIAL OF A NUMBER

In mathematics, the factorial of a non-negative integer n denoted by $n!$, is the product of all positive integers less than or equal to n. For example:

$$6! = 6 \times 5 \times 4 \times 3 \times 2 \times 1 = 720$$

Input

The first line of the input contains an integer N ($1 \leq N \leq 5$), the number of test cases. Following the first line are the test cases. Each line in a test case contains a non-negative integer number.

The input must be read from standard input.

Output

The output of the program should print the result of the factorial of the numbers.

The output must be written to standard output.

Sample Input	Sample Output
3 6 7 8	720 5040 40320

POSSIBLE SOLUTION: FACTORIAL OF A NUMBER *(C++)*

```cpp
#include <iostream>
#include<conio.h>

using namespace std;

int main()

{

    // Variable Declaration

    int counter, n, N, x;
    int numbers[5];

    // Get Input Value

    cin>>N;

    for (x=0; x<N; x++)
    {
    cin>>n;

    //for Loop Block
    int fact = 1;
    for (int counter = 1; counter <= n; counter++)
    {
        fact = fact * counter;
        numbers[x] = fact;

    }
    }

    cout<<endl;
    for (x = 0; x<m; x++)
        cout<<numbers[x]<<"\n";

    // Wait For Output Screen

    getch();

    return 0;

}
```

PROBLEM 5 : THE SQUARE MATRIC

In mathematics, a square matrix is a matrix with a same number of rows and columns. An *n-by-n* matrix is known as a square matrix of order *n*. For instance, this is square matrix of order 3:

$$\begin{pmatrix} 4 & 2 & 1 \\ 5 & 3 & 2 \\ 6 & 8 & 7 \end{pmatrix}$$

Write a program that is able to display a square matrix of any order as specified by the user. All the entries of the matrix are 1s except the entries in the main diagonal and anti-diagonal. The entries in both diagonals should be 0s.

Input
Any integer number.

Output
The square matrix of any order as specified by the user with its entries in principal diagonal and anti-diagonal is 0s. The rest of the entries remain to be 1s.

Sample Input	Sample Output
7	0 1 1 1 1 1 0 1 0 1 1 1 0 1 1 1 0 1 0 1 1 1 1 1 0 1 1 1 1 1 0 1 0 1 1 1 0 1 1 1 0 1 0 1 1 1 1 1 0
4	0 1 1 0 1 0 0 1 1 0 0 1 0 1 1 0

33

POSSIBLE SOLUTION 3 : THE SQUARE MATRIX *(C++)*

```cpp
#include<iostream>
using namespace std;

int main()
{
    int no_order;

    cin>>no_order;

    for (int row = 0; row < no_order; row++)
    {
        for (int column = 0; column < no_order; column++)
        {
            if (column == row)
                cout<<"0 ";
            else if (row + column == no_order - 1)
                cout<<"0 ";
            else
                cout<<"1 ";
        }
        cout<<endl;
    }
    system("pause");
    return 0;
}
```

PROBLEM 6: PALINDROME NUMBER

A **palindrome** is a word, phrase, number, or other sequence of characters, which reads the same backward or forward.

Input
User need to enter 5 digit number and program will determine whether the number is palindrome or not.

Output
The program will display the results whether the number is a palindrome number or not.

Sample input 1	Sample output 1
12345	12345 is not palindrome number.

Sample input 2	Sample output 2
12521	12521 is palindrome number

POSSIBLE SOLUTION: PALINDROME NUMBER (C++)

```cpp
#include<iostream>
#include<fstream>
using namespace std;
int main()
{
    int num,A,B,C,D,E,rem;

    cin>>num;
    A=num/10000;
    rem=num%10000;
    B=rem/1000;
    rem=rem%1000;
    C=rem/100;
    rem=rem%100;
    D=rem/10;
    rem=rem%10;
    E=rem;

    if ((A==E)&&(B==D))
        cout<<num<<" is palindrome number.";
    else
        cout<<num<<" is not palindrome number.";
```

PROBLEM 7: SHADED REGION

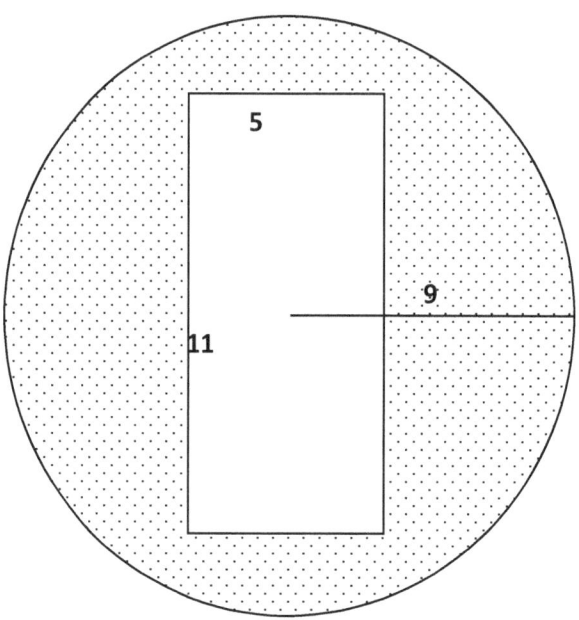

Given the figure above, find the shaded region.

Input
User is required to input the radius of the circle, length and width of the rectangle (separated by spaces).

Output
The program will display the area of the shaded region.

Sample input	Sample output
9 11 5	254.502
	55
	199.502

POSSIBLE SOLUTION: SHADED REGION *(C++)*

```cpp
#include<iostream>

using namespace std;

int main()
{
    float rad, pi = 3.142, l, w, area_circle, area_rectangle,
    shaded_region;

    cin>>rad>>l>>w;

    area_circle = pi * rad * rad;
    area_rectangle = l * w;

    shaded_region = area_circle - area_rectangle;

    cout<<area_circle<<endl;
    cout<<area_rectangle<<endl;
    cout<<shaded_region<<endl;

    system("pause");
}
```

PROBLEM 8: LEXICOGRAPHIC ORDERING

When comparing two strings using lexicographic (dictionary) ordering, corresponding letters are compared until one of the string ends or the first difference is encountered.

If one of the strings ends, the longer string is considered the later one. If a character mismatch is found, compare the characters to determine which string comes later in the sequence.

Input

The first line of the input contains the number of strings to be tested. Following the first line are the test cases. Each line in a test case contains a string with maximum 30 characters.

For example,

3
Tomato
Tony
Tom

The input must be read from standard input.

Output

The output of the program should print the strings in lexicographic order.

The output must be written to standard output.

Sample Input	Sample Output
4 compute comparison compete computer	comparison compete compute computer

39

POSSIBLE SOLUTION: LEXICOGRAPHIC ORDERING *(C++)*

```
#include <iostream.h>
#include<string.h>

void main()
{
     int i,j,numWords;
     char string[10][30], temp[30];
     cin>>numWords;

     for (i=0; i<numWords; i++)
     {
          cin>>string[i];
     }

     for (i=0; i<numWords; i++)
     {
          for (j=(i+1); j<numWords; j++)
          {
                     if(strcmp(string[i],string[j])>0)
                     {
                          strcpy(temp,string[i]);
                          strcpy(string[i], string[j]);
                          strcpy(string[j], temp);
                     }
          }
     }
     cout<<endl;
     for (i=0; i<numWords; i++)
     {
          cout<<string[i]<<endl;
     }

}
```

PROBLEM 9: ADD & REVERSE

In order to apply for the post of a programmer at Setia Indah Software House, candidates are required to solve the following problem.

	1	4	5	6

+

Sum of two numbers

	2	5	6	7

	3	9	11	13

Display results in reverse order

	13	11	9	3

Input
User is required to input 8 numbers. The program will pair first 4 numbers with the next 4 numbers and find sum of the paired numbers.

Output
The program will display the results in reverse order.

Sample input 1	Sample output 1
1 2 3 4 2 8 2 7	115103

Sample input 2	Sample output 2
4 7 2 9 4 3 5 2	117108

POSSIBLE SOLUTION: ADD & REVERSE *(C++)*

```cpp
#include <iostream>

using namespace std;

int main()
{

int num1[4];
int num2[4];
int sum[4];
int x,y,z,a;

for(x=0;x<=3;x++)
{
cin>>num1[x];
}

for(y=0;y<=3;y++)
{
cin>>num2[y];
}

for(z=0;z<=3;z++)
{
sum[z]=num1[z]+num2[z];
}

for(a=3;a>=0;a--)
{

cout<<sum[a];
}


}
```

PROBLEM 10: ENCRYPTION

There are many ways to do encryption. This is my way of encrypting data. Every vowel in a word will be change to as follows:

Vowel	Encrypted code
a	*
e	#
i	@
o	~
u	?

Input
A word less than 10 characters.
Output
The output will display the encrypted word.

Sample Input	Sample Output
program software database	pr~gr*m s~ftw*r# s~ftw*r#

POSSIBLE SOLUTION: ENCRYPTION *(C++)*

```cpp
#include<iostream>
usingnamespacestd;

int main()
{
char word[10];

cin>>word;

for(inti =0; i<10; i++)
{
if(word[i]=='a')
        word[i] = '*';
if(word[i]=='e')
        word[i] = '#';
if(word[i]=='i')
        word[i] = '@';
if(word[i]=='o')
        word[i] = '~';
if(word[i]=='u')
        word[i] = '?';
 }
cout<<word;
}
```